I0528806

GRANDMA MARGIE'S TALE THE PROMISE OF THE SEVEN COLOR RAINBOW.

Written by **Dr. K.T. Zulkowski**

Copyright © 2023 by Dr. K.T. Zulkowski

All rights reserved. No part of this book may be reproduced or transmitted in any form or by anymeans, electronic or mechanical, including photocopying, recording, or by any information storage and retrieval system, without permission in writing from the publisher.

Published by Mz. Kim Productions
4263 Tierra Rejada Rd #151
Moorpark, CA 93021
www.mzkimproductions.com

ISBN: 978-1-962106-17-7

Printed in United States of America
First Printing: August 2023
Date of Copyright: July 5,2023

For permissions, please contact: Mz. Kim Productions
4263 Tierra Rejada Rd #151
Moorpark, CA 93021
www.mzkimproductions.com
mzkimproductions@gmail.com

The characters and events portrayed in this book are fictitious. Any similarity to real persons, living or dead, is purely coincidental and not intended by the author.

Dedication

To my beloved Christian community, This book is dedicated to all of you, my fellow brothers and sisters in Christ, with deep love and unwavering faith. As we embark on this journey together, I want to proclaim the significance of the rainbow as a symbol of God's promise specifically for us, His chosen people. In the pages that follow, we will explore the story of Grandma Margie and the Promise of the Rainbow, delving into the biblical account of Noah's Ark and the covenant God made with His people. Through vibrant illustrations and heartfelt words, I aim to remind each one of you of the profound meaning behind the rainbow and its connection to our Christian faith. Just as God promised never to flood the earth again, He has made countless promises to us as His children. The rainbow serves as a constant reminder of His faithfulness, love, and protection. It is a symbol that belongs to us, the followers of Christ, as a testament to the covenant we have with our Heavenly Father. As we turn the pages of this book, may it ignite a renewed sense of hope and assurance in your hearts. May it strengthen your faith and remind you of the promises God has made to us through His Word. Let the colors of the rainbow be a vivid reminder of His grace, mercy, and unending love for each one of us. I am honored to share this journey with you, my dear Christian community. May this book serve as a beacon of light, guiding us closer to God's promises and inspiring us to live lives that reflect His glory. With heartfelt love and unwavering faith,

Dr. K.T. Zulkowski

Educational Value

This book offers several educational benefits for young readers:

1. Introduction to Biblical Stories: Through the story of Noah's Ark, children are introduced to a well-known Bible story and learn about God's promise to never flood the earth again.

2. Understanding Symbolism: Children learn about the symbolism of the seven color rainbow and how it represents God's love, faithfulness, and protection.

3. Colors and Visual Perception: The book explores the seven colors of the rainbow, helping children recognize and identify them. The vibrant illustrations enhance their understanding of colors and visual perception.

4. Appreciation for Nature: The book encourages children to appreciate the beauty of nature, including rainbows, flowers, and the world around them.

5. Family Bonding and Values: The strong bond between Grandma Margie and her grandchildren highlights the importance of family relationships and passing down values and teachings from one generation to another.

6. Spiritual Development: The book fosters spiritual development by introducing children to the concept of God's promises and His presence in their lives, promoting a sense of security and trust.

Overall, "Grandma Margie and the Promise of the Rainbow" combines storytelling, colorful illustrations, and educational elements to teach children about the significance of the rainbow and God's promises in a fun and engaging way.

Grandma Margie: "Hello, my dear Zipporah and Zion! Today, I want to tell you about a very special promise that God made long ago."

Grandma Margie: "In the Bible, there is a story about a man named Noah. God sent a great flood, but Noah and his family were saved on an ark filled with animals."

Zipporah: "Wow, Grandma Margie! Look at that colorful rainbow! It's so pretty!"

Grandma Margie: "Yes, Zipporah, rainbows are beautiful. But they are also a special sign from God."

Grandma Margie: "Do you see the colors of the rainbow? There are seven colors: red, orange, yellow, green, blue, indigo, and violet."

Zion: "Grandma Margie, why did God make the rainbow?"

Génesis 9:13. : I have set my rainbow in the clouds, and it will be the sign of the covenant between me and the earth.

Grandma Margie: "God made the rainbow as a promise to never flood the whole earth again. It's a sign of His love and faithfulness."

Zipporah: "So, whenever we see a rainbow, it means God loves us and keeps His promises?"

Grandma Margie: "Exactly, Zipporah! Rainbows remind us that God always keeps His promises, just like He promised to send Jesus to save us."

Zion: "I love rainbows, Grandma Margie! They make me feel happy and safe."

Grandma Margie: "Rainbows are a reminder of God's love and protection. Whenever you see one, remember that God is always with you."

Zipporah: "Thank you, God, for the beautiful rainbow and for always keeping your promises. Amen."

Grandma Margie: "Now, let's go outside and enjoy the sunshine and the colors of the world that God has created for us."

Zion: "Look, Grandma Margie! Our garden is like a rainbow on the ground!"

Grandma Margie: "God's promise of the rainbow is a reminder to always be thankful for His love and the beautiful world He has given us."

Zipporah: "I love you, Grandma Margie! And I love God's promise of the rainbow too!"

Grandma Margie: "Remember, my dear ones, whenever you see a rainbow, think of God's love and His promises. He will always be with you."

Zion: "Goodnight, Grandma Margie. Thank you for teaching us about the rainbow and God's promises."

Grandma Margie: "You're welcome, my sweethearts. I will always be here to remind you of God's love and the promise of the rainbow."

Grandma Margie: "Sleep tight, my little ones. May God's love and the promise of the rainbow fill your dreams."

Grandma Margie: "Good morning, my precious ones! Let's start a new day, knowing that God's promises are always true."

Zipporah: "Thank you, Grandma Margie, for teaching us about the rainbow and God's promises. We will always remember."

Grandma Margie: "And I will always be here to remind you, my dear ones. God's promises are forever."

Zion: "We love you, Grandma Margie! And we love God's promise of the rainbow!"

Grandma Margie: "I love you too, my sweethearts! And I'm so grateful for God's promise of the rainbow. It reminds us of His love and faithfulness, always."

Author's Note

Dear readers,

It is with great joy and excitement that I present to you "Grandma Margie and the Promise of the Rainbow." As a children's book author and a believer in the power of storytelling, it has been my privilege to create this heartwarming tale that explores the significance of the rainbow and God's promises.

Growing up, I was always captivated by the beauty of rainbows and the sense of wonder they evoked. As I delved deeper into the Bible, I discovered the story of Noah's Ark and the promise that God made to never flood the earth again. This promise, symbolized by the seven color rainbow, became a powerful reminder of God's love and faithfulness.

In writing this book, my aim was to share this message of hope and assurance with young readers. Through the character of Grandma Margie, I wanted to portray the wisdom and love that grandparents often impart to their grandchildren. By incorporating dialogue, illustrations, and references to scriptures, I hope to engage children in a meaningful way and help them understand the significance of the rainbow and God's promises.

I believe that children's books have the power to shape young minds and hearts. They can instill values, foster imagination, and provide a foundation for spiritual growth. It is my sincere hope that "Grandma Margie and the Promise of the Rainbow" accomplishes these goals and leaves a lasting impact on the lives of its readers.

I would like to express my gratitude to the talented illustrators who brought this story to life with their vibrant and enchanting artwork. Their illustrations beautifully complement the narrative and capture the essence of the rainbow's beauty.

Lastly, I would like to thank you, dear readers, for embarking on this journey with Grandma Margie, Zipporah, and Zion. May this book inspire you to appreciate the wonders of nature, embrace God's promises, and cherish the love of family the way God designed the family to be.

With warmest regards,

Dr. K.T. Zulkowski

www.ingramcontent.com/pod-product-compliance
Lightning Source LLC
Chambersburg PA
CBHW041431120626
46547CB00002B/174